christmas at home

Festive
FINGER FOODS

AMY ROBERTSON

BARBOUR
PUBLISHING

© 2003 by Barbour Publishing, Inc.

ISBN 1-59310-043-4

Cover image © Getty Images

Scripture quotations are taken from the King James Version of the Bible.

Published by Barbour Publishing, Inc., P.O. Box 719, Uhrichsville, Ohio 44683, www.barbourbooks.com

Our mission is to publish and distribute inspirational products offering exceptional value and biblical encouragement to the masses.

Printed in Canada.
5 4 3 2

contents

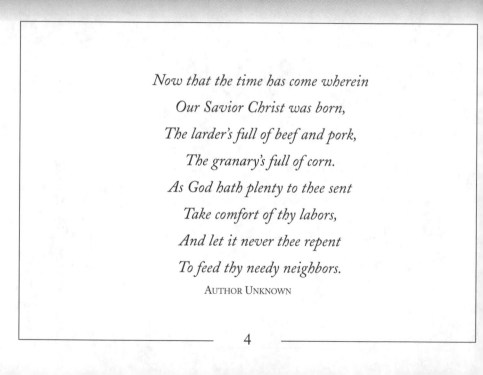

Now that the time has come wherein

Our Savior Christ was born,

The larder's full of beef and pork,

The granary's full of corn.

As God hath plenty to thee sent

Take comfort of thy labors,

And let it never thee repent

To feed thy needy neighbors.

AUTHOR UNKNOWN

Appetizers & Dips

For unto you is born this day in the city of
David a Saviour, which is Christ the Lord.

LUKE 2:11

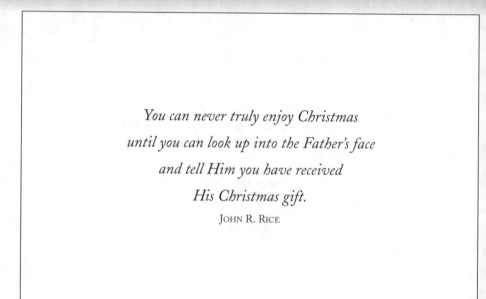

You can never truly enjoy Christmas
until you can look up into the Father's face
and tell Him you have received
His Christmas gift.

JOHN R. RICE

Christmas PARTY POTATOES

15 small red potatoes
½ cup sour cream

Dill weed sprigs or chopped chives

Bring 1 inch of water to a boil in 3-quart saucepan. Add potatoes. Cover and reduce heat. Simmer 20–25 minutes, or until potatoes are tender. Drain and cool. Cut potatoes in half, and place cut sides facing up on a serving tray or plate. Cut a thin slice from the bottom of each potato half, if necessary, to help it stand upright. Top each potato half with 1 teaspoon of sour cream and a dill weed sprig. Cover and refrigerate until potatoes are chilled.

Holiday BRUSCHETTA

2 large tomatoes, chopped
½ sweet onion, chopped
2 tablespoons olive oil
1 clove garlic, crushed
1 tablespoon fresh oregano, chopped

1 teaspoon fresh basil, chopped
2 teaspoons fresh parsley, chopped
½ loaf Italian bread, cut into 1-inch squares
¾ cup grated Parmesan cheese

Preheat oven to 400 degrees. In a medium bowl, combine tomatoes, onion, olive oil, garlic, oregano, basil, and parsley. Line a cookie sheet with aluminum foil. Place bread on the foil and top with the tomato mixture. Sprinkle with Parmesan cheese. Bake for 8–10 minutes or until bread is browned. Allow to cool before serving.

Cocktail MEATBALLS

1 pound ground beef
½ cup dry bread crumbs
⅓ minced onion
¼ cup milk
1 egg
1 tablespoon snipped parsley

1 teaspoon salt
⅛ teaspoon pepper
½ teaspoon Worcestershire sauce
¼ cup shortening
1 (12-ounce) bottle chili sauce
1 (10-ounce) jar grape jelly

In a large bowl, mix ground beef, bread crumbs, onion, milk, egg, parsley, salt, pepper, and Worcestershire sauce. Gently shape into 2-inch balls. In a large skillet, melt shortening. Add meatballs and cook until brown. Remove from skillet and drain. Heat chili sauce and jelly in skillet, stirring constantly until jelly is melted. Add meatballs and stir until thoroughly coated. Simmer uncovered for 30 minutes.

Broccoli SQUARES

2 (8-ounce) cans refrigerated
crescent roll dough
2 (8-ounce) packages cream
cheese, softened
1 cup mayonnaise

1 (1-ounce) package ranch
dressing mix
1 head fresh broccoli, chopped
3 Roma (plum) tomatoes, chopped
1 cup cheddar cheese, shredded

Preheat oven to 375 degrees. Lightly grease a baking sheet. Arrange the crescent roll dough in 4 rectangles on the baking sheet. Bake in the preheated oven for 12 minutes or until golden brown. Remove from heat and allow to cool completely. In a medium bowl, mix the cream cheese, mayonnaise, and dry ranch dressing mix. Spread evenly over the crescent rolls. Sprinkle with broccoli and tomatoes. Top with cheddar cheese and serve.

Cheesy POTATO SKINS

4 large potatoes
2 tablespoons butter or margarine,
    melted
1 cup shredded Colby-
    Monterey Jack or cheddar cheese

8 (½ cup) medium green onions,
    sliced
½ cup sour cream

Preheat oven to 375 degrees. Pierce potatoes to allow steam to escape. Bake 60–75 minutes, or until potatoes are tender. Let stand until cool enough to handle. Cut potatoes lengthwise into fourths. Carefully scoop out some of the centers, leaving ¼-inch shells. Set oven control to broil. Place potato shells, skin sides down, on rack in broiler pan. Brush skins with butter. Broil potatoes with the tops 4–5 inches from heat for about 5 minutes, or until potatoes are crispy. Sprinkle cheese over potatoes. Broil an additional 30–45 seconds, or until cheese is melted. Serve hot with green onions and sour cream.

Sweet POTATO BALLS

1 (40-ounce) can sweet potatoes
1/4 cup butter
1 pinch salt

3 cups cornflakes cereal, crushed
3/4 cup maple syrup
10 large marshmallows

Preheat oven to 325 degrees. Grease a 9x13-inch baking dish. Drain sweet potatoes and place into a large bowl. Mash the potatoes and add the butter; mix well. Add salt to taste. Roll the mixture into 3-inch balls. Roll each ball in the crushed cereal. Place balls in prepared baking dish. Pour maple syrup evenly over all balls. Bake for 40 minutes in preheated oven. For the last 15 minutes, place a marshmallow on each ball.

Cocktail WEINERS

1 (10-ounce) jar chili sauce   2 packages smoked cocktail wieners
1 small jar grape jelly

Preheat oven to 350 degrees. In a small saucepan, combine chili sauce and jelly. Heat until well blended. In a casserole dish, place the cocktail wieners. Pour jelly mixture over wieners. Bake for 15–20 minutes.

Bacon-Wrapped HOT DOGS

2–3 packages hot dogs
2 pounds bacon

Toothpicks
2 pounds brown sugar, packed

Slice hot dogs into thirds. Cut bacon slices into thirds. Wrap each hot dog with a cut piece of bacon and hold in place with a toothpick. Place wrapped hot dogs into a Crock-Pot until it is full. Pour brown sugar over the hot dogs. Cook on low for 3–4 hours.

Sweet-n-Sour COCKTAIL LINKS

1 pound cocktail links
2 cups ketchup
2 tablespoons mustard

¾ cup orange juice
¾ cup brown sugar, packed
1 tablespoon onion, grated

In a large skillet, combine cocktail links, ketchup, mustard, orange juice, brown sugar, and onion. Simmer over low heat for about 30 minutes. Serve hot.

Mushroom STUFFED TRIANGLES

¼ pound fresh mushrooms,
   coarsely chopped
2 tablespoons minced fresh parsley
2 tablespoons minced onion
3 tablespoons butter, divided

1 (8-ounce) can refrigerated
   crescent roll dough
2½ tablespoons grated Parmesan
   cheese
2 tablespoons sesame seeds

Preheat oven to 375 degrees. In a medium saucepan, over medium heat, cook the mushrooms, parsley, and onion in 2 tablespoons of butter until tender; stirring frequently. Drain and set aside. Separate the dough into 4 rectangles. Cut each rectangle in half, forming 8 squares. Arrange the squares on a large baking sheet. Place 1 tablespoon of the mushroom mixture on each square. Top each mushroom-covered square with 1 teaspoon of Parmesan cheese. Fold the squares into triangles. Melt the remaining butter in the microwave. Brush triangles with the butter and sprinkle with sesame seeds. Bake in the preheated oven for 10–15 minutes, or until triangles are golden brown. Serve warm.

Barbecued CHICKEN WINGS

3 pounds chicken wings
1 clove garlic, crushed
Celery salt to taste
2 tablespoons butter, melted

1 tablespoon lemon juice
Pepper to taste
1 cup hot sauce

Preheat the broiler or grill. Prepare the chicken wings. Combine the garlic, celery salt, butter, lemon juice, and pepper in a small bowl. Brush the wings with this mixture. Arrange the chicken wings on the grill or in the broiler and begin cooking them. Baste them after the first 5 minutes and every subsequent 5 minutes until the wings are completely cooked.

Sausage BALLS

$1/2$ pound fresh, ground pork sausage
$1/2$ pound fresh, ground spicy pork sausage
2 ounces processed cheese sauce
2 cups buttermilk biscuit mix

Preheat oven to 325 degrees. In a medium bowl, combine regular sausage, spicy sausage, cheese sauce, and biscuit mix. Mix well and form into 1-inch balls. Place on a cookie sheet. Bake 15–20 minutes.

Stuffed DEVILED EGGS

6 hard-boiled eggs, peeled
¼ cup mayonnaise
2 tablespoons bacon bits
2 teaspoons lemon juice
1½ teaspoons Worcestershire sauce

1 teaspoon mustard
¼ teaspoon salt
⅛ teaspoon pepper
Parsley
Paprika

Cut eggs lengthwise in half. Remove the yolks and place them in a small bowl. Place the sliced egg white halves on a plate; set aside. Mash the yolks with a fork. Stir in the mayonnaise, bacon bits, lemon juice, Worcestershire sauce, mustard, salt, and pepper. Fill the egg white halves with the egg yolk mixture, heaping it slightly. Garnish with parsley and paprika.

Deviled EGGS

6 eggs
1 teaspoon white vinegar
2 tablespoons mayonnaise
1/4 teaspoon mustard

Salt and pepper to taste
1 1/2 teaspoons paprika
2 leaves lettuce

Place eggs in a pot with 3 inches of water. Add a few dashes of salt. Bring the water to a boil, and cook eggs in the boiling water for about 10–15 minutes or until hard-boiled. Drain the eggs and place on a paper towel to cool. Once they are cool, peel off the shells, and cut the eggs in half lengthwise. Scoop out all of the yolks. Place all of the yolks in a medium bowl and mash them. Add the vinegar, mayonnaise, mustard, salt and pepper; stir until well blended. Carefully put spoonfuls of the egg yolk mixture back into each egg. Sprinkle paprika over the yolks in each egg. Place on a bed of lettuce. Cool before serving.

Pecan Stuffed MUSHROOMS

20 medium-sized mushrooms
3 tablespoons butter, melted
3 ounces cream cheese, softened
2 tablespoons bacon, cooked
    and crumbled

1 1/2 tablespoons chopped pecans
2 tablespoons Italian-style
    bread crumbs
2 teaspoons minced chives

Gently separate stems from mushroom caps. Brush mushroom caps
with the melted butter. Fill each cap with a mixture of cream cheese,
bacon, pecans, bread crumbs, and chives. Broil stuffed mushrooms for
3–5 minutes. Serve hot.

Garlic PICKLED EGGS

12 eggs
1 onion, sliced into rings
1 cup distilled white vinegar
1 cup water

¼ cup sugar
10 cloves garlic, peeled
Salt to taste

Place eggs in a medium saucepan and cover with water. Bring water to a boil and immediately remove from heat. Cover and let eggs stand in the hot water for 10–12 minutes. Remove from water, cool, and peel. Place eggs in a 1-quart jar with the onions. In a medium saucepan, add the vinegar, water, sugar, and garlic. Bring to a boil, then remove from heat and allow to cool for 15 minutes. Pour the vinegar mixture over the eggs and cover. Refrigerate for at least one week before serving.

Tomato BACON ROLLS

8 slices bacon
1 tomato, chopped
½ onion, chopped
3 ounces mozzarella cheese,
 shredded

1 ounce Parmesan cheese, shredded
¼ cup mayonnaise
1 teaspoon dried basil
1 can refrigerated crescent roll dough

Preheat oven to 375 degrees. In a skillet, over medium heat, cook bacon until evenly browned. Drain the bacon on paper towels. Crumble the bacon into small pieces in a medium mixing bowl. Add tomato, onion, cheese, mayonnaise, and basil; mix well. Unroll the dough, and place a spoonful of the tomato mixture in the center of each piece of roll. Roll up each piece of dough, with the mixture inside. Place on an ungreased baking sheet and bake in preheated oven for 11–14 minutes or until golden brown.

Chicken QUESADILLAS

1 skinless, boneless chicken breast,
    cut into strips
1 tablespoon vegetable oil
1 small onion, chopped

3 tablespoons salsa
10 (10-inch) flour tortillas
2 cups shredded Colby-Monterey
    Jack cheese

Preheat oven to 350 degrees. Spray a cookie sheet with a nonstick cooking spray. In a large skillet, add the vegetable oil. Fry the chicken strips until they are no longer pink. Add the onion and fry, stirring constantly. Add the salsa; stir well. Place the tortillas between two damp paper towels and microwave on high (100%) for 1 minute. Spread some of the chicken mixture over half the side of one tortilla. Sprinkle cheese over the mixture. Fold the tortilla in half. Repeat with the remaining tortillas. Arrange the tortillas on the prepared cookie sheet. Bake until cheese is melted. Cut the quesadillas into fourths.

Pickled PUMPKIN

4 pounds pumpkin, peeled and diced
5 cups sugar
5 cups distilled white vinegar

4 cinnamon sticks
15 whole cloves

Place the pumpkin pieces in a large bowl; set aside. In a large saucepan, combine the sugar, vinegar, cinnamon sticks, and cloves. Bring to a boil, and boil for 5 minutes, stirring occasionally. Pour the hot vinegar mixture over the pumpkin. Cover and allow to set overnight. Strain the liquid into a large saucepan. Boil for 5 minutes. Remove the cinnamon sticks and cloves; leave a few for decoration. Place the pumpkin back into the liquid and return to boiling. Boil for 5 minutes, or until the pumpkin is transparent and crisp. Allow the mixture to cool. Transfer to jars and refrigerate.

Cream Cheese PENGUINS

18 jumbo black olives, pitted
1 (8-ounce) package cream cheese,
   softened

1 carrot
18 small black olives

Cut a slit from top to bottom, lengthwise, into the side of each jumbo olive. Carefully insert about 1 teaspoon of cream cheese into each olive. Slice the carrot into eighteen ¼-inch-thick rounds; cut a small notch out of each carrot slice to form feet. Save the cutout pieces and press one into the center of each small olive to form the beak. If necessary, cut a small slit into each olive before inserting the beak. Set a jumbo olive, large hole side down, onto a carrot slice. Then, set a small olive onto the large olive, adjusting so that the beak, cream cheese chest, and notch in the carrot slice line up. Secure with a toothpick.

Baked CREAM CHEESE

½ (8-ounce) package refrigerated
    crescent roll dough
1 (8-ounce) package cream cheese,
    softened

½ teaspoon dried dill weed
1 egg yolk, beaten

Unroll crescent roll dough on a lightly floured surface; press together seams to form a 12x4-inch rectangle. Sprinkle one side of the cream cheese with half of the dill weed. Place brick of cream cheese dill side down in the center of the dough. Sprinkle the remaining dill on top of cream cheese. Enclose the cream cheese by bringing the sides of the dough together and pressing edges to seal. Place dough on lightly greased cookie sheet. Brush with beaten egg yolk. Bake at 350 degrees for 15–18 minutes. Cut into slices and serve warm.

Christmas CHEESE BALL

(8-ounce) cream cheese
4 ounces blue cheese
1 tablespoon green pepper, chopped

1 tablespoon diced pimento
Chopped walnuts
Minced parsley

In a medium bowl, combine cream cheese, blue cheese, green pepper, and pimento. Roll into a ball. Roll the ball in the chopped walnuts. Garnish with parsley and serve with crackers.

Chocolate Chip CHEESE BALL

1 (8-ounce) package
    cream cheese, softened
$\frac{1}{2}$ cup butter, softened
$\frac{3}{4}$ cup powdered sugar
2 tablespoons brown sugar,
    firmly packed

$\frac{1}{4}$ teaspoon vanilla extract
$\frac{3}{4}$ cup miniature semisweet
    chocolate chips
$\frac{3}{4}$ cup finely chopped pecans

In a medium bowl, combine cream cheese and butter. Beat with an electric hand mixer, on low speed, until smooth. Stir in powdered sugar, brown sugar, and vanilla. Add chocolate chips; stir. Cover and refrigerate for 2 hours. Form the chilled mixture into the shape of a ball. Wrap in plastic wrap and refrigerate for another hour. Roll the ball in the chopped pecans. Keep refrigerated until ready to serve.

Chicken CHEESE BALL

2 (8-ounce) packages cream cheese, softened

1 (1-ounce) package ranch dressing mix

1 (5-ounce) can chunk white chicken, drained

½ cup pecans, chopped

In a medium bowl, combine cream cheese, ranch dressing mix, and chicken. Form the mixture into a ball. On a piece of waxed paper, spread out the chopped pecans. Roll the ball in the pecans until it is completely coated. Wrap in plastic and refrigerate for at least one hour.

Pepperoni CHEESE BALL

4 (3-ounce) packages cream
    cheese, softened
1/4 cup mayonnaise
1/8 teaspoon garlic powder

1/3 cup Parmesan cheese
1/2 teaspoon oregano
1 (8-ounce) package pepperoni,
    chopped

In a large bowl, combine cream cheese, mayonnaise, garlic powder,
Parmesan cheese, oregano, and pepperoni; mix well. Form mixture into a ball.
Chill in the refrigerator for at least 24 hours. Serve cold with crackers.

Pumpernickel SPINACH DIP

1 (8-ounce) container sour cream
½ (8-ounce) package cream cheese, softened
2 tablespoons mayonnaise
1 (1-ounce) package dill dip mix
½ bunch spinach, rinsed and chopped
1 (8-ounce) round pumpernickel loaf

In a medium bowl, combine the sour cream, cream cheese, mayonnaise, dill dip mix, and spinach; mix well. Cut out the center of the pumpernickel loaf, creating a bowl. Cut the removed bread into bite-sized squares. Fill the hollowed loaf with the spinach dip. Serve with the pumpernickel squares.

Pumpkin DIP

1 (8-ounce) package cream cheese, softened
2 cups powdered sugar
1 (15-ounce) can solid-pack pumpkin
1 tablespoon ground cinnamon
1 tablespoon pumpkin pie spice
1 teaspoon frozen orange juice concentrate

In a medium bowl, combine cream cheese and sugar; mix until smooth. Stir in the pumpkin. Add the cinnamon, pumpkin pie spice, and orange juice. Mix until well blended. Chill in the refrigerator 1 hour before serving. Hollow a miniature pumpkin and place dip inside just before serving. Serve with apple wedges and gingersnaps.

Holiday BEAN DIP

2 (11-ounce) cans white corn, drained
2 (15-ounce) cans black beans, rinsed and drained
1/2 cup Italian salad dressing
1 cup ranch salad dressing

1 small onion, chopped
1 teaspoon hot pepper sauce
2 teaspoons fresh cilantro, chopped
1 teaspoon chili powder
1/2 teaspoon ground black pepper

In a medium bowl, thoroughly mix white corn, black beans, Italian salad dressing, ranch salad dressing, onion, hot pepper sauce, cilantro, chili powder, and ground black pepper. Chill in the refrigerator overnight before serving. Serve cold with tortilla chips or crackers.

Christmas Tree DIP

1 (8-ounce) package cream cheese,
  softened
1 yellow bell pepper
1 (2-inch) piece green onion

¼ cup salsa
¼ cup apricot preserves
1 teaspoon fresh cilantro, chopped

Cut the block of cream cheese diagonally in half. Arrange the cut cream cheese triangles on a serving plate to form a tree. Cut a star shape out of the bell pepper with a small star-shaped cookie cutter. Place the star at the top of the tree. Place the green onion piece at the bottom of the tree to form the trunk. In a small bowl, mix together the salsa and the apricot preserves. Spoon the mixture over the cream cheese tree. Sprinkle cilantro over the tree. Serve with tortilla chips or crackers.

Corn Chip DIP

1 large can refried beans
1 package taco seasoning mix
1 (8-ounce) container sour cream

1 can black olives, chopped
2 cups shredded cheddar cheese

In a small bowl, combine beans and taco mix. Spread over the bottom of a microwave-safe dish. Cover with sour cream. Sprinkle olives and cheese over top. Microwave on high (100%) until cheese is melted. Serve hot with corn chips.

Pineapple CREAM CHEESE DIP

2 (8-ounce) packages
   cream cheese, softened
1 cup minced celery
½ cup green bell pepper, chopped

1 teaspoon minced onion
1 (20-ounce) can crushed
   pineapple, drained
1 cup chopped pecans

In a medium mixing bowl, combine cream cheese, celery, bell pepper, onion, and crushed pineapple; mix well. Stir in the chopped pecans. Chill in the refrigerator overnight. Serve with crackers.

Hot Onion DIP

3 (8-ounce) packages cream cheese, softened
1 onion, finely chopped

2 cups grated Parmesan cheese
1/2 cup mayonnaise

Preheat oven to 400 degrees. Lightly grease a medium baking dish. Place the cream cheese, onion, cheese, and mayonnaise in the prepared dish; mix well. Bake in the preheated oven for 30 minutes or until lightly browned and bubbly. Serve hot with your favorite crackers.

Roasted RED PEPPER DIP

1 (7-ounce) jar roasted red peppers, drained and diced
¾ pound shredded Monterey Jack cheese
1 (8-ounce) package cream cheese, softened
1 cup mayonnaise
1 tablespoon onion, minced
1 clove garlic, minced
2 tablespoons prepared Dijon mustard
Salt and pepper to taste

Preheat oven to 350 degrees. Place the roasted red peppers, Monterey Jack cheese, cream cheese, mayonnaise, onion, garlic, and mustard in a small baking dish; mix well. Bake in the preheated oven for 20 minutes, or until lightly browned and bubbly. Serve warm with tortilla chips.

Avocado DIP

2 ripe avocados
½ cup mayonnaise
¾ cup cheddar cheese, grated

1 cup sour cream
2 tablespoons lemon juice

Combine all of the above ingredients in a medium bowl. Beat with an electric hand mixer, on low speed, for 2 minutes. Cover and refrigerate before serving. Serve with tortilla chips or party crackers.

Spicy Nacho CHEESE DIP

1 (1-pound) hot sausage roll
1 (10-ounce) can nacho cheese soup

2 (10-ounce) cans
   cheddar cheese soup
Jalapenos to taste, chopped

Preheat oven to 350 degrees. In a large skillet, brown and crumble sausage over medium heat; drain. In a casserole dish, combine cooked sausage, undiluted nacho soup and cheddar soup, and jalapenos; stir. Bake in preheated oven for 20–25 minutes. Serve with tortilla chips.

Christmas SHRIMP DIP

1 (10-ounce) can tomato soup
½ (8-ounce) package cream cheese, softened
1 envelope gelatin
½ cup water

1 cup mayonnaise
½ cup onion, chopped
½ cup celery, chopped
Baby shrimp

In a small saucepan, cook undiluted soup; melt cream cheese in it. In a separate saucepan, dissolve gelatin in water. Add mayonnaise, onion, and celery to the soup mixture. Stir in the gelatin mixture and refrigerate overnight. Serve cold with baby shrimp.

Simple CRAB DIP

1 block cream cheese, softened
   (room temperature)
1 onion, diced

1 can crabmeat, drained
Cocktail sauce

In a medium bowl, combine cream cheese, onion, and crabmeat; mix well. Spoon the mixture onto the center of a serving tray, and spread with cocktail sauce over top. Surround the dip with crackers.

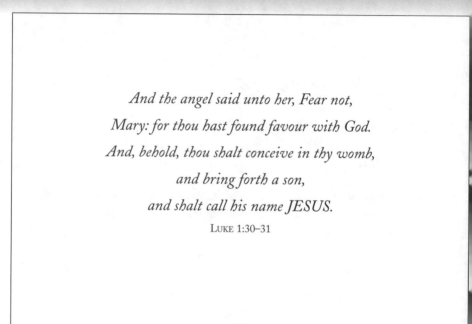

And the angel said unto her, Fear not,
Mary: for thou hast found favour with God.
And, behold, thou shalt conceive in thy womb,
and bring forth a son,
and shalt call his name JESUS.

LUKE 1:30–31

Holiday Breads & Rolls

Good news from heaven the angels bring,

Glad tidings to the earth they sing:

To us this day a child is given,

To crown us with the joy of heaven.

MARTIN LUTHER

Banana Nut BREAD

4 cups all-purpose flour
1 1/4 cups nonfat dry milk
4 teaspoons baking powder
1 teaspoon cinnamon
4 large eggs

3 1/2 cups ripe bananas, mashed
2 cups sugar
1 cup vegetable oil
1 cup chopped walnuts

Preheat oven to 350 degrees. Grease two 9x5-inch loaf pans. Stir together flour, dry milk, baking powder, and cinnamon in a medium bowl. In a large mixing bowl, add the eggs, bananas, sugar, and oil. With an electric hand mixer on medium speed, beat the banana mixture until it is completely blended. Gradually beat in the flour mixture. Stir in the walnuts. Spoon the mixture into prepared loaf pans. Bake for 60–65 minutes or until toothpick inserted in center comes out clean. Cool in pans for 10 minutes. Remove to wire racks to cool completely.

Chocolate Chip PUMPKIN BREAD

3 cups powdered sugar
1 (15-ounce) can solid-pack
   pumpkin
1 cup vegetable oil
²/₃ cup water
4 eggs
3½ cups all-purpose flour

1 tablespoon ground cinnamon
1 tablespoon ground nutmeg
2 teaspoons baking soda
1½ teaspoons salt
1 cup miniature semisweet chocolate chips
½ cup walnuts, chopped
   (optional)

Preheat oven to 350 degrees. Grease and flour three 1-pound-size coffee cans or three 9x5-inch loaf pans. In a large bowl, combine sugar, pumpkin, oil, water, and eggs. Beat until smooth. Blend in flour, cinnamon, nutmeg, baking soda, and salt. Fold in chocolate chips and nuts. Fill cans or loaf pans $\frac{1}{2}$–$\frac{3}{4}$ full. Bake for 1 hour or until a toothpick inserted in the center comes out clean. Cool on wire racks before removing from cans or loaf pans. Makes 3 loaves.

Zucchini BREAD

2 eggs
2 cups sugar
1 cup oil
1 tablespoon vanilla extract
2 cups zucchini, grated
1 teaspoon baking soda

1 teaspoon salt
3 cups flour
1/4 teaspoon baking powder
1 tablespoon cinnamon
1/2 cup chopped nuts
1/2 cup raisins

Preheat oven to 325 degrees. Grease and flour two loaf pans; set aside. In a large bowl, add eggs, sugar, and oil. Beat with an electric hand mixer on low speed until well blended. Add vanilla and grated zucchini. Sift and add dry ingredients. Stir in nuts and raisins. Pour batter into prepared pans. Bake for 45–60 minutes or until toothpick inserted in center comes out clean.

Apple BREAD

$1/3$ cup butter or margarine, softened

$3/4$ cup sugar

1 teaspoon baking soda

1 tablespoon lemon juice

2 eggs

1 teaspoon vanilla extract

2 tablespoons flour

$1/4$ teaspoon salt

$1 1/2$ cups apples, peeled and chopped

1 teaspoon cinnamon

$1 1/2$ cups flour

2 tablespoons sugar

2 tablespoons butter

Preheat oven to 325 degrees. Grease and flour a 9x5-inch loaf pan; set aside. In a small bowl, cream together butter and sugar. In a separate bowl, dissolve baking soda in lemon juice. Mix in eggs and vanilla. Beat butter mixture and egg mixture together. Add flour and salt. Be careful not to overmix. Gently stir in apples. In a small bowl, add cinnamon, 2 tablespoons flour, and 2 tablespoons sugar. Cut in 2 tablespoons butter to get a coarse crumb mixture; set aside. Spoon $\frac{1}{2}$ apple batter into prepared loaf pan. Sprinkle with $\frac{1}{2}$ crumb mixture. Spoon in remaining batter and sprinkle with remaining crumb mixture. Press crumbs gently into surface of batter. Bake for 80–90 minutes or until a toothpick inserted in the center comes out clean. Cool for 10 minutes in pan before turning out onto a wire rack. Allow to cool completely before slicing.

Cranberry NUT BREAD

2 cups all-purpose flour
¾ cup powdered sugar
¾ teaspoon salt
1½ teaspoons baking powder
½ teaspoon baking soda
1 cup cranberries, chopped

½ cup nuts, chopped
1 egg
2 tablespoons vegetable oil
¾ cup orange juice
1 tablespoon orange peel, grated

Preheat oven to 350 degrees. Grease a 9x5-inch loaf pan. In a large bowl, combine the flour, sugar, salt, baking powder, and baking soda. Add the cranberries and nuts. Stir to coat with the flour. In a small bowl, combine the egg, oil, orange juice, and grated orange peel; stir. Add the egg mixture to the flour mixture and stir until combined. Pour the batter into the prepared pan. Bake for 50–60 minutes or until a toothpick inserted into the center comes out clean. Let cool for 10 minutes before removing from the pan and placing on a cooling rack. Cool for 60 minutes before slicing.

Holiday PUMPKIN BREAD

1 (15-ounce) can solid-pack pumpkin
4 eggs
1 cup vegetable oil
²⁄₃ cup water
3 cups sugar
3¹⁄₂ cups all-purpose flour

2 teaspoons baking soda
1¹⁄₂ teaspoons salt
1 teaspoon ground cinnamon
1 teaspoon ground nutmeg
¹⁄₂ teaspoon ground cloves
¹⁄₄ teaspoon ground ginger

Preheat oven to 350 degrees. Grease and flour two 9x5-inch loaf pans. In a medium bowl, combine pumpkin, eggs, oil, water, and sugar; mix until well blended. In a large bowl, whisk together the flour, baking soda, salt, cinnamon, nutmeg, cloves, and ginger. Add the dry ingredients to the pumpkin mixture and stir until blended. Pour into the prepared pans. Bake for 50–60 minutes or until toothpick inserted in the center comes out clean. Makes 2 loaves.

Strawberry BREAD

2½ cups fresh strawberries
3⅛ cups all-purpose flour
2 cups powdered sugar
1 tablespoon ground cinnamon
1 teaspoon salt

1 teaspoon baking soda
1¼ cups vegetable oil
4 eggs, beaten
1¼ cups chopped pecans

Preheat oven to 350 degrees. Butter and flour two 9x5-inch loaf pans. Slice the strawberries, and place them in a medium bowl. Sprinkle sugar lightly over them and set aside. Mix the flour, sugar, cinnamon, salt, and baking soda in a large bowl. Stir the oil and eggs into the bowl with the strawberries. Add the strawberry mixture to the flour mixture; stir well. Add the pecans; stir. Divide the batter and pour into the two prepared pans. Bake for 45–60 minutes, or until toothpick inserted in the center comes out clean. Let cool in pans for 10 minutes before turning loaves out. Cool completely on wire rack before slicing.

Cinnamon BREAD

2 cups flour
1 cup sugar
2 teaspoons baking powder
1/2 teaspoon baking soda
1 1/2 teaspoons ground cinnamon
1 teaspoon salt
1 cup buttermilk

1/4 cup vegetable oil
2 eggs
2 teaspoons vanilla extract
2 tablespoons sugar
1 teaspoon ground cinnamon
2 teaspoons margarine

Preheat oven to 350 degrees. Grease a 9x5-inch loaf pan. In a large mixing bowl, combine flour, 1 cup sugar, baking powder, baking soda, 1½ teaspoons cinnamon, salt, buttermilk, oil, eggs, and vanilla. Beat with an electric hand mixer on low speed for 3 minutes. Pour mixture into the prepared loaf pan. Smooth the top with a spatula. In a small bowl, combine 2 tablespoons sugar, 1 teaspoon cinnamon, and margarine, stirring until crumbly. Sprinkle topping over smoothed batter. Using a knife, cut through the topping in a light swirling motion to give a marbled effect. Bake for 45–50 minutes, or until toothpick inserted in the center comes out clean. Allow to cool for 10 minutes before removing bread from pan. Allow to cool completely on wire rack before slicing.

Monkey BREAD

1 cup sugar

2 teaspoons ground cinnamon

3 (12-ounce) packages refrigerated
biscuit dough

$\frac{1}{2}$ cup chopped walnuts (optional)

$\frac{1}{2}$ cup raisins (optional)

$\frac{1}{2}$ cup margarine

1 cup brown sugar, packed

Preheat oven to 350 degrees. Grease a 9-inch tube pan. Combine sugar and cinnamon in a plastic bag. Cut biscuits into quarters. Shake 6–8 biscuit pieces at a time in the sugar-cinnamon mixture. Arrange the pieces in the bottom of the prepared pan. Continue until all biscuits are coated and placed in the pan. If using nuts and raisins, arrange them in the biscuit pieces as you go along. In a small saucepan, over medium heat, melt the margarine with the brown sugar. Boil for 1 minute. Pour the mixture over the biscuits. Bake for 35 minutes. Let bread cool in pan for 10 minutes, then turn the bread out onto a plate. Do not cut; pull bread apart.

Peanut Butter BREAD

¾ cup sugar

½ cup peanut butter

1 teaspoon vanilla extract

1¾ cups milk

2¼ cups flour

4 teaspoons baking powder

½ teaspoon salt

Preheat oven to 350 degrees. Grease and flour a 9x5-inch loaf pan. In a large bowl, cream together the sugar, peanut butter, and vanilla. Add the milk and mix well. In a medium bowl, combine flour, baking powder, and salt; stir. Add the flour mixture to the peanut butter mixture and beat well. Pour batter into prepared pan. Bake for 50 minutes, or until a toothpick inserted into the center comes out clean.

Cheddar BISCUITS

4 cups all-purpose baking mix
3 ounces cheddar cheese, shredded
1 1/3 cups water
1/2 cup butter, melted

1 teaspoon garlic powder
1/4 teaspoon salt
1/8 teaspoon onion powder
1/8 teaspoon dried parsley

Preheat oven to 375 degrees. Line a baking sheet with a piece of parchment paper. In a large mixing bowl, combine the baking mix, cheese, and water. Mix ingredients until the dough is firm. Using a small scoop or a spoon, place the dough on the prepared pan. Bake for 10–12 minutes or until golden brown. In a small bowl, combine the melted butter, garlic powder, salt, onion powder, and parsley; mix well. Brush over baked biscuits immediately upon removing from the oven.

Cinnamon CRESCENT ROLLS

1 (8-ounce) can refrigerated crescent roll dough
¾ cup cinnamon chips
⅓ cup powdered sugar
½ tablespoon ground cinnamon

Preheat oven to 375 degrees. Unroll dough and separate into triangles. Sprinkle cinnamon chips evenly over the triangles. Gently press the cinnamon chips into the dough and roll up. Place the rolls on an ungreased cookie sheet. Bake 10–12 minutes or until rolls are golden brown. Sprinkle with powdered sugar and cinnamon. Serve warm.

The Christmas Gift

The Christmas Season speaks
    to us of peace
A season of solace and joy.
When eager children must wait
    endless hours
To examine their new Christmas toys.
The family will gather for breaking
    of bread
Thanking God for their bountiful food,
Then thanking each other for gifts
    they exchanged
As they bask in a joyful mood.
However, most cherished of all
    of their gifts
Is a gift they can't visibly see.

This endowment is offered to one
    and to all
But is not to be found 'neath the tree.
It's a blessing bestowed to all
    of mankind
God Himself is in it reflected
It carries the power to alter his life,
If man simply opts to accept it.
This gift is the reason we celebrate
On Christmas the wee infant's birth
For God has appeared in a human form
To walk among men on the earth.

AUTHOR UNKNOWN

And so it was, that, while they were there,
the days were accomplished that she should be delivered.
And she brought forth her firstborn son,
and wrapped him in swaddling clothes,
and laid him in a manger;
because there was no room for them in the inn.

LUKE 2:6–7

sandwiches & snacks

And this shall be a sign unto you; Ye shall find the babe
wrapped in swaddling clothes, lying in a manger.

LUKE 2:12

Flaky SANDWICH SLICES

1 (15-ounce) package refrigerated
    piecrusts, softened
½ cup grated Parmesan cheese

½ pound thin sliced ham
¼ pound thin sliced pepperoni
1 cup shredded cheddar cheese

Preheat oven to 450 degrees. Remove the crusts from the package and unfold them. Sprinkle the Parmesan cheese over each crust. Place a layer of ham, pepperoni, and cheddar cheese over each crust within 1 inch of the edges. Roll up each crust and place rolls, with the seam side facing down, on an ungreased cookie sheet. Fold the ends under. Bake for 13–15 minutes or until golden brown. Let cool before cutting into slices.

Ham AND *Basil* PINWHEELS

1 (8-ounce) package cream cheese,
    softened
6 (10-inch) flour tortillas
12 slices ham

4 ounces fresh basil
1 cup sun-dried tomatoes
12 leaves red leaf lettuce, rinsed
Toothpicks

Lightly spread cream cheese over each tortilla. Arrange two slices of ham across the center of each cream cheese-covered tortilla. Add a layer of fresh basil and then a layer of tomatoes. Leave $\frac{1}{2}$ inch around the edges of the tortilla. Add the lettuce. Tightly roll up each tortilla. Secure with toothpicks in four evenly spaced spots of the tortilla roll. Place rolls in baking dish, cover, and refrigerate for at least 2 hours. Slice each roll into four evenly sized sandwich slices. Arrange on a serving tray and serve cold.

Cheese AND *Onion* ROLL-UPS

1 cup sour cream
1 (8-ounce) package cream cheese,
    softened
½ cup shredded cheddar cheese
¾ cup green onions, sliced

1 tablespoon lime juice
1 tablespoon jalapeno peppers,
    seeded and minced
10 (6-inch) flour tortillas

In a medium bowl, mix the sour cream, cream cheese, cheddar cheese, green onions, lime juice, and jalapeno peppers. Spread one side of each tortilla with the mixture. Tightly roll up each tortilla. Place rolled tortillas in a baking dish and cover. Refrigerate for at least one hour. Slice tortillas into 1-inch slices. Arrange on a tray and serve with salsa.

Christmas TOSTADAS

1 pound hamburger
1 package taco seasoning mix
6 small flour tortillas
1 green pepper, seeded and diced

1 tomato, diced
½ cup black olives, sliced
3 cups lettuce, shredded
6 ounces sliced Monterey Jack
    cheese, cut into strips

Preheat oven to 350 degrees. Line a cookie sheet with aluminum foil; set aside. Prepare hamburger with taco seasoning mix according to package directions. Cut tortillas into Christmas tree shapes using a cookie cutter. With a spoon, spread $\frac{1}{3}$ cup of the hamburger mixture evenly over each tortilla. Leave a $\frac{1}{2}$-inch border of tortilla all the way around each one. Use the green pepper, tomato, black olives, and lettuce to decorate the tortillas like Christmas trees. Arrange the cheese on each tortilla in a zigzag pattern to make it look like garland. Use a spatula to place each tortilla on the prepared cookie sheet. Bake for 5–8 minutes, or until cheese is melted. Top with sour cream and taco sauce if desired.

Mini PARTY KABOBS

½ pound fully cooked kielbasa, cut into ½-inch pieces
1 (10-ounce) jar red or green maraschino cherries, drained
1 (5-ounce) jar small green olives
1 (8-ounce) packaged processed cheese cubes
Toothpicks

On each toothpick, place one piece of sausage, one cherry, one olive, and one cube of cheese. Arrange them neatly on a serving tray.

Holiday TURKEY ROLL

1 pound cream cheese, softened   ½ pound smoked turkey, sliced thin
12 (10-inch) flour tortillas   1 head lettuce
¾ cup jellied cranberry sauce

Spread a thin layer of cream cheese over each tortilla. Spread 1 tablespoon of cranberry sauce onto the cream cheese layer. Cover the cranberry sauce with two thin slices of turkey. Top the turkey with a single layer of lettuce. Roll up the tortilla and wrap in aluminum foil. Refrigerate for 1 hour. Cut into 1-inch slices.

Holiday CHICKEN SALAD SANDWICHES

1 cup mayonnaise
1 teaspoon paprika
1 teaspoon seasoned salt
1½ cups dried cranberries
1 cup celery, chopped
½ cup green pepper, minced

2 green onions, chopped
1 cup chopped pecans
4 cups cooked chicken breast, cubed
Ground black pepper to taste
Croissants

In a medium mixing bowl, combine the mayonnaise with paprika and seasoned salt. Add the dried cranberries, celery, green pepper, onion, and pecans; stir well. Mix in the cubed chicken. Season with black pepper. Chill in the refrigerator for 1 hour before serving. Serve on croissants.

Bite-Size TACO TURNOVERS

½ pound ground beef
¼ cup taco sauce
2 teaspoons chili powder
¼ teaspoon onion powder
¼ teaspoon garlic powder

1 (10-ounce) package refrigerated
   pizza dough
¼ cup shredded cheddar cheese
1 egg
1 teaspoon water

Preheat oven to 425 degrees. Cook ground beef in a small skillet until brown; drain. Stir in taco sauce, chili powder, onion powder, and garlic powder; set aside. Unroll pizza dough. Roll dough into a 14x10 1/2-inch rectangle. Cut into twelve 3 1/2-inch squares. Divide the filling among the dough squares. Sprinkle with cheese. Brush edges with water. Lift the corner of each square and stretch the dough to the opposite corner, making a triangle. Press edges with a fork to seal. Arrange the triangles on a greased baking sheet. Prick with a fork. In a small bowl, combine the egg and water. Brush onto the triangles. Bake for 8–10 minutes or until golden. Let stand 5 minutes before serving.

Ham ROLLS

5 slices cooked ham
1 (8-ounce) package cream cheese,
    softened

5 green onions
Toothpicks

Lay the ham slices on a flat surface and spread with cream cheese. Place one green onion on each slice of ham. Roll the ham slices up tightly. Cut into bite-sized pieces and pierce each piece with a toothpick. Arrange neatly on a serving tray.

Chicken FINGERS

4 (4-ounce) skinless,
    boneless chicken breasts
1 cup flour
½ teaspoon salt

¼ teaspoon pepper
¾ cup milk
1 cup vegetable oil for frying

Cut the chicken into ½x2-inch strips. Mix the flour, salt, and pepper in a shallow bowl. Dip the chicken into the milk, then roll in the flour mixture; coat well. Place coated chicken on waxed paper. Pour ¼ inch of the oil into a large skillet. Heat over medium-high heat. Divide chicken into batches of 10–12 pieces. Place chicken in an even layer in the hot oil. Fry, turning once, for about 3 minutes on each side or until golden brown and crispy. Drain on paper towels and serve with barbecue or honey mustard sauce.

Red-Hot CHICKEN BITES

3 pounds boned chicken breasts
1/8 teaspoon garlic salt
2 tablespoons red pepper

1/2 teaspoon black pepper
1 cup flour
Vegetable oil

Cut chicken breasts lengthwise into 1-inch pieces. Sprinkle garlic salt over chicken, turning pieces so each gets evenly coated. Continue with red pepper, then black pepper. Set aside for 1 hour to allow the chicken to absorb flavor. Dust each chicken piece with flour, then deep fry in vegetable oil at 375 degrees for 3 minutes. Drain on paper towels and serve warm.

Cheese STRAWS

½ cup butter, softened
4 cups shredded cheddar cheese
2 cups flour

1 teaspoon salt
¼ teaspoon ground red pepper
(optional)

Preheat oven to 400 degrees. Grease a cookie sheet; set aside. In a large bowl, combine the butter and cheese; mix well. Stir in the flour and salt. On a lightly floured surface, roll the dough out to ½-inch thickness. Cut dough into 2-inch strips and sprinkle with red pepper. Place the strips on the prepared cookie sheet 1½ inches apart. Bake for 10–15 minutes or until crisp.

Corn FRITTERS

3 cups oil for frying
1 cup flour
1 teaspoon baking powder
1/2 teaspoon salt
1/4 teaspoon sugar

1 egg
1/2 cup milk
1 tablespoon shortening, melted
1 (12-ounce) can whole kernel
    corn, drained

Heat oil in a heavy pot or a deep fryer to 365 degrees. In a medium bowl, combine flour, baking powder, salt, and sugar. In a small bowl, beat together the egg, milk, and melted shortening. Stir the egg mixture into the flour mixture. Stir in the corn and mix well. Drop the fritter batter by spoonfuls into the hot oil. Fry until golden brown. Drain fritters on paper towels. Serve warm.

One day has left its mark in time
For all mankind to see;
It is the day when Christ was born—
That day made history.

D. DeHaan

Party Trays & Mixes

Come to Bethlehem and see
Him whose birth the angels sing;
Come adore on bended knee
Christ the Lord, the newborn King.

TRADITIONAL FRENCH CAROL

Sweet PARTY MIX

1 (12-ounce) package
   crispy corn and rice cereal
5 ounces slivered almonds
6 ounces toasted, chopped pecans

¾ cup butter
¾ cup dark corn syrup
1½ cups light brown sugar

Preheat oven to 250 degrees. Lightly grease a large roasting pan. In a large bowl, mix cereal, almonds, and pecans. In a medium saucepan, over medium heat, melt the butter and add corn syrup and brown sugar; stir. Pour the butter mixture over the cereal mixture; toss to coat evenly. Pour the mixture into the prepared pan. Bake for 1 hour, stirring every 15 minutes. Allow to cool and store in an airtight container.

Holiday SNACK MIX

2 cups salted peanuts
$\frac{1}{2}$ cup whole almonds
$\frac{1}{2}$ cup cashews
$\frac{1}{2}$ cup chopped dates

$\frac{1}{2}$ cup red and green candy-coated
    chocolate pieces
$\frac{1}{2}$ cup raisins
2 tablespoons shelled sunflower seeds

Combine all ingredients in a large bowl; mix well. Store in an airtight container in a cool, dry place.

Christmas PARTY MIX

2 cups miniature pretzels
2 cups chow mein noodles
2 cups crispy corn squares cereal
1 cup peanuts
1 cup raisins
3 egg whites

1 ½ cups sugar
1 teaspoon ground cinnamon
1 teaspoon salt
1 large package candy-coated
   chocolate pieces

Preheat oven to 225 degrees. Grease a cookie sheet; set aside. In a large bowl, combine the pretzels, chow mein noodles, cereal, peanuts, and raisins. In a medium bowl, beat egg whites until foamy. Stir in the sugar, cinnamon, and salt. Pour over the pretzel mixture, and stir until evenly coated. Spread onto prepared cookie sheet. Bake for 1 hour, turning mix with a spatula every 15 minutes. Allow to cool completely. Stir in the chocolate pieces. Store in an airtight container in a cool, dry place.

Popcorn PARTY MIX

3 quarts popcorn, popped
1 cup unsalted dry-roasted peanuts
1 jar (3½ ounces) macadamia
   nuts, halved
½ cup slivered almonds
¼ cup flaked coconut
¾ cup butter (no substitutes)

1 cup sugar
½ cup brown sugar, firmly packed
¼ cup light corn syrup
¼ cup strong brewed coffee
⅛ teaspoon cinnamon
2 teaspoons vanilla extract

Preheat oven to 250 degrees. Grease two 10x15x1-inch baking pans; set aside. Combine popcorn, nuts, and coconut in a large bowl. Combine the butter, sugars, corn syrup, coffee, and cinnamon in a medium saucepan. Bring to a boil over medium heat. Boil, stirring constantly for 5 minutes. Remove from heat and stir in the vanilla. Pour over the popcorn mixture and stir until well coated. Transfer to the prepared baking pans. Bake, uncovered, for 45–55 minutes or until golden brown, stirring every 15 minutes. Immediately spread onto the waxed paper and let stand until completely cooled. Break apart into small pieces. Store in an airtight container.

Ranch PRETZELS

1 (20-ounce) package thick pretzels
1 envelope ranch dressing mix
1½ teaspoons dill weed

1½ teaspoons garlic powder
(optional)
¾ cup vegetable oil

Preheat oven to 200 degrees. Grease a 10x15x1-inch baking pan; set aside. Break pretzels into bite-sized pieces and place in a large bowl. In a small bowl, combine remaining ingredients and pour over pretzels. Stir well to coat. Pour pretzels into prepared pan. Bake for 1 hour, stirring every 15 minutes. Allow to cool and store in an airtight container.

Frosted PECAN BITES

1 pound pecan halves
2 egg whites, stiffly beaten
1 cup sugar

Pinch of salt
1/2 cup butter

Preheat oven to 275 degrees. Place the pecans on a cookie sheet and toast for 10–15 minutes; set aside to cool. Place egg whites in a medium bowl. Fold in sugar, salt, butter, and the toasted pecans. Increase oven temperature to 325 degrees. Grease the cookie sheet and spread the pecan mixture over it. Bake for 30 minutes, stirring every 10 minutes. Allow to cool completely before serving.

Orange SPICED NUTS

3 cups pecan halves
1 cup sugar
$\frac{1}{3}$ cup orange juice

1 tablespoon ground cinnamon
$\frac{1}{2}$ teaspoon salt
$\frac{1}{2}$ teaspoon ground cloves

Spread the pecans over the bottom of a 10x15x1-inch pan. Toast at 275 degrees for 10 minutes. Remove from the oven and set aside. In a medium saucepan, combine the sugar, orange juice, cinnamon, salt, and ground cloves. Over medium heat, cook and stir until heat reaches the soft-ball stage. Remove from heat and stir in the pecans. Remove the pecans from the pan and spread onto waxed paper. Separate and let dry for 2 hours. Store in an airtight container.

Favorite PARTY MIX

½ cup butter
2 tablespoons Worcestershire sauce
1½ teaspoons seasoned salt
½ teaspoon garlic powder
½ teaspoon onion powder

3 cups crispy corn squares cereal
1 cup cashews
1 cup miniature pretzels
1 cup garlic-flavored bagel chips

Preheat oven to 250 degrees. Melt butter in large roasting pan in oven for 5 minutes. Stir in Worcestershire sauce, seasoned salt, garlic powder, and onion powder. Add remaining ingredients and gently stir until evenly coated. Bake for 1 hour, stirring every 15 minutes. Spread on paper towels to cool, and store in an airtight container.

Caramel POPCORN

3 quarts popcorn, popped
3 cups mixed nuts, unsalted
1 cup brown sugar, firmly packed
1/2 cup light corn syrup

1/2 cup margarine
1/2 teaspoon salt
1/2 teaspoon baking soda
1/2 teaspoon vanilla extract

Preheat oven to 250 degrees. In a large roasting pan, combine the popcorn and nuts. Place pan in the oven while preparing the glaze. In a medium saucepan, combine brown sugar, corn syrup, margarine, and salt. Bring to a boil over medium heat, stirring constantly. Boil for 4 minutes without stirring. Remove from heat; stir in baking soda and vanilla. Pour the mixture over the warm popcorn and nuts, tossing to coat evenly. Bake another 60 minutes, stirring every 10–15 minutes. Cool and break apart. Store in an airtight container.

Butterscotch Crispy PARTY MIX

2 cups rice squares cereal
2 cups small pretzel twists
1 cup dry-roasted peanuts

1 cup caramels, unwrapped,
    coarsely chopped
1 (11-ounce) package butterscotch chips

Coat a 9x13-inch baking pan with nonstick cooking spray. In a large bowl, combine the cereal, pretzel twists, peanuts, and caramels. Place the butterscotch chips in a medium microwave-safe bowl. Microwave at high (100%) for 1 minute; stir. Microwave an additional 10–20 seconds or until smooth when stirred. Pour over the cereal mixture; stir to coat evenly. Spread the mixture into the prepared baking pan; let stand for 20–30 minutes or until mixture is firm. Break apart into small pieces.

 *Taco* SNACK MIX

4 cups crispy corn squares cereal
4 cups small pretzel sticks
4 cups tortilla chips

1 package taco seasoning
¼ cup margarine, melted

In a large bowl, combine the cereal, pretzel sticks, tortilla chips, and taco seasoning; toss until evenly coated with seasoning. Drizzle melted margarine over mix and toss to coat well. Store in an airtight container in a cool, dry place.

Spiced MIXED NUTS

1 egg white, lightly beaten
1 teaspoon water
1 (8-ounce) jar dry-roasted peanuts
½ cup blanched whole almonds

½ cup pecan halves
¾ cup sugar
1 tablespoon pumpkin pie spice

In a large bowl, combine egg white and water. Add nuts; toss to coat. Combine sugar and spice; sprinkle over the nuts and toss until well coated. Place nuts in a single layer on lightly greased baking sheet. Bake at 300 degrees for 20–25 minutes. Immediately transfer the nuts to waxed paper. Allow to cool. Break up any large clusters. Store in an airtight container.

Roasted PUMPKIN SEEDS

1 1/2 cups raw whole pumpkin seeds   Pinch of salt
2 teaspoons butter, melted

Preheat oven to 300 degrees. In a small bowl, toss seeds with melted butter and salt. Spread the seeds in a single layer on a cookie sheet. Bake for 45–50 minutes or until golden brown, stirring occasionally. Allow to cool before serving. Hollow a miniature pumpkin and place roasted seeds inside just before serving.

Spicy PUMPKIN SEEDS

1 1/2 tablespoons margarine, melted
1/2 teaspoon salt
1/8 teaspoon garlic salt

2 teaspoons Worcestershire sauce
2 cups raw whole pumpkin seeds

Preheat oven to 275 degrees. In a small bowl, combine the melted margarine, salt, garlic salt, Worcestershire sauce, and pumpkin seeds; toss to coat well. Place seeds in a shallow baking dish. Bake for 1 hour, stirring occasionally.

Glazed NUTS

1 egg white
½ cup brown sugar, packed
2 tablespoons ground cinnamon
1 teaspoon ground cloves
1 teaspoon ground ginger

1 tablespoon vanilla extract
1 cup walnut halves
1 cup pecans
1 cup almonds

Preheat oven to 300 degrees. Spray a cookie sheet with nonstick cooking spray. In a large bowl, beat egg white until foamy. Stir in the brown sugar, cinnamon, cloves, ginger, and vanilla. Add the nuts; stir to coat. Spread evenly onto the prepared cookie sheet. Bake for 30 minutes, stirring occasionally, until golden brown. Allow to cool completely. Store in an airtight container.

Cinnamon-Roasted ALMONDS

1 egg white
1 teaspoon cold water
4 cups whole almonds

$\frac{1}{2}$ cup sugar
$\frac{1}{4}$ teaspoon salt
$\frac{1}{2}$ teaspoon ground cinnamon

Preheat oven to 250 degrees. Lightly grease a 10x15x1-inch pan. Lightly beat the egg white; add water, and beat until frothy but not stiff. Add the almonds and stir until well coated. In a small bowl, combine the sugar, salt, and cinnamon; sprinkle over the almonds. Toss to coat, and spread evenly on the prepared pan. Bake for 1 hour, stirring occasionally, until golden. Allow to cool completely. Store in an airtight container.

Christmas PARTY HAM RING

1 envelope unflavored gelatin
$\frac{1}{4}$ cup cold water
1 cup sour cream
$\frac{1}{2}$ cup mayonnaise
3 tablespoons vinegar
$\frac{1}{4}$ teaspoon salt

Pepper to taste
$1\frac{1}{2}$ cups ham, cooked, diced
1 cup celery, sliced
$\frac{1}{4}$ cup parsley, chopped
3 tablespoons green onion,
    chopped

In a medium saucepan, soften gelatin in water; bring to a boil. Blend in sour cream, mayonnaise, vinegar, salt, and pepper. Chill until thickened; whip until fluffy. Fold in the ham, celery, parsley, and green onion. Pour into $5\frac{1}{2}$-cup ring mold. Chill until firm. Turn onto a serving tray and serve with crackers.

Holiday Party CHEESE WREATH

2 (8-ounce) packages cream
  cheese, softened
8 ounces shredded mild
  cheddar cheese
1 tablespoon red pepper, chopped

1 tablespoon green onion,
  finely chopped
2 tablespoons Worcestershire sauce
1 tablespoon lemon juice
Dash of ground red pepper

In a large bowl, mix cream cheese and cheddar cheese with an electric hand mixer on medium speed until well blended. Add red pepper, onion, Worcestershire sauce, lemon juice, and ground pepper; mix well. Refrigerate overnight. Place a drinking glass in the center of a serving tray. Drop rounded tablespoons of cheese mixture around the glass, just touching the rim to form a ring. Smooth out with a spatula or spoon. Remove glass. Garnish with fresh parsley and serve with holiday crackers.

Holiday BREAD TRAY

½ loaf banana nut bread, sliced
½ loaf pumpkin bread, sliced
½ loaf cranberry bread, sliced

½ loaf cinnamon bread, sliced
Butter or margarine
Cinnamon-flavored butter

Cut each slice of bread into 1-inch squares. Spread ⅓ of the bread squares with regular butter, ⅓ with cinnamon butter and leave remaining squares plain. Place the bread squares on a holiday serving tray. Garnish with pieces of fruit and nuts if desired.

Festive Fruits & Vegetables

And it came to pass, as the angels were gone
away from them into heaven, the shepherds
said one to another, Let us now go even
unto Bethlehem, and see this thing which is
come to pass, which the Lord hath made
known unto us. And they came with haste,
and found Mary, and Joseph, and the babe
lying in a manger.

Luke 2:15–16

What can I give Him,
Poor as I am?
If I were a shepherd
I would bring a lamb.
If I were a Wise Man
I would do my part.
Yet what can I give Him?
I give Him my heart.

CHRISTINA ROSSETTI

Christmas FRUIT DIP

1 (7-ounce) jar marshmallow cream
¼ cup powedered sugar
1 tablespoon lemon juice

(8-ounce) package cream
    cheese, softened

In a medium bowl, beat all ingredients together until well blended. Serve as a party dip. Arrange whole or sliced fruits on a party tray around the bowl of dip.

Caramel APPLE BITES

6 individually wrapped caramels,
    unwrapped and chopped

2 tablespoons light corn syrup
2 apples, peeled, cored, and diced

Combine the caramels and corn syrup in a medium, microwave-safe bowl. Microwave on high (100%) for about 30 seconds or until melted. Put the apples in the bowl and toss until coated with the caramel mixture. Allow to cool 10 minutes before serving.

Festive FRUIT KABOBS

½ (20-ounce) can sliced pineapple
    in juice, drained
16 seedless red grapes
16 toothpicks

16 seedless green grapes
1 (10-ounce) jar maraschino
    cherries, drained

Cut pineapple slices into eighths. Thread any combination of 4–5 pieces of fruit on each of 16 toothpicks. Serve with your favorite fruit dip.

Fruit PIZZA

1 roll refrigerated sugar cookie dough
3-ounce package cream
   cheese, softened
$1/3$ cup brown sugar, firmly packed

1 cup sour cream
$1/2$ teaspoon vanilla extract
4 cups assorted fresh fruit,
   sliced

Preheat oven to 350 degrees. Press sugar cookie dough into an ungreased 12-inch pizza pan. Bake for 10–15 minutes or until golden. Cool. Combine cream cheese, brown sugar, sour cream, and vanilla in a medium bowl. Beat with an electric hand mixer on low speed until smooth. Spread mixture over cooled cookie crust evenly. Arrange sliced fruit on top. Refrigerate until ready to serve.

Strawberry FRUIT DIP

1 (8-ounce) package strawberry-flavored cream cheese
1 (7-ounce) jar marshmallow crème

In a medium mixing bowl, mix the cream cheese and marshmallow crème until well blended. Chill at least one hour before serving. Serve with your favorite fruit.

Mango CREAM CHEESE PIZZA

1 ready-made pizza crust
1 tablespoon olive oil
1 (13½-ounce) container fruit-flavored cream cheese
1 (26-ounce) jar mango slices, drained and chopped
½ cup chopped walnuts

Bake pizza crust according to package directions. Brush crust with olive oil. Spread cream cheese over the crust. Arrange the mango slices over the cream cheese and sprinkle with walnuts. Slice and serve.

Fruit SALSA

2 kiwifruit, peeled and diced
2 apples, peeled, cored, and diced
8 ounces raspberries
1 pound strawberries

2 tablespoons powdered sugar
1 tablespoon brown sugar,
    firmly packed
3 tablespoons fruit preserves,
    any flavor

In a large bowl, mix kiwifruit, apples, raspberries, strawberries, powdered sugar, brown sugar, and fruit preserves. Cover and refrigerate. Serve with cinnamon chips (see page 141 for recipe).

Cinnamon CHIPS

10 (10-inch) flour tortillas   2 cups cinnamon sugar
Butter-flavored cooking spray

Preheat oven to 350 degrees. Coat one side of each flour tortilla with the butter-flavored cooking spray. Cut the tortillas into wedges and arrange them in a single layer on a large cookie sheet. Sprinkle the wedges with the cinnamon sugar. Spray them once more with the butter-flavored cooking spray. Bake for 8–10 minutes. Repeat the process with any remaining tortilla wedges. Allow to cool for at least 15 minutes. Serve with the fruit salsa (see page 140 for recipe).

Honey Yogurt FRUIT DIP

1 container vanilla yogurt
3 tablespoons honey

Fresh fruit such as apples, pears,
grapes, strawberries, and kiwifruit

Place the yogurt in medium bowl; whisk until smooth. Stir in the honey, leaving a marbled effect. Cut the fruit into wedges or bite-sized pieces, or leave whole. Arrange the fruit on a platter with the bowl of dip in the center. Serve chilled.

 FRUIT DIP

1 (3-ounce) package instant vanilla
    pudding mix
1½ cups milk

1 (6-ounce) can frozen
    orange juice concentrate
¼ cup sour cream
¼ teaspoon ginger

In a medium bowl, combine pudding mix, milk, and orange juice concentrate; mix well for 1 minute. Stir in sour cream and ginger. Chill several hours to blend flavors. Serve with fresh fruit for dipping.

Coffee FRUIT DIP

1 (8-ounce) package cream
   cheese, softened
1 (8-ounce) container sour cream
½ cup brown sugar, firmly packed

⅓ cup coffee
1 (8-ounce) container frozen
   whipped topping, thawed

Place cream cheese, sour cream, brown sugar, and coffee in a medium bowl. Blend together with an electric mixer until smooth. Fold in whipped topping. Chill in refrigerator until served.

Caramel FRUIT DIP

1 (8-ounce) package cream cheese   ½ cup caramel topping
¼ cup honey   ¼ teaspoon cinnamon

Let cream cheese soften in a medium-sized mixing bowl about 15 minutes, or until mixer can blend it easily. Add remaining ingredients and beat until smooth and creamy. Serve with fresh fruit.

Hot JEZEBEL

1 (12-ounce) jar apricot preserves
2 tablespoons prepared horseradish
2 tablespoons Dijon mustard

Ground black pepper to taste
1 (8-ounce) package cream cheese, softened

In a medium-size bowl, combine apricot preserves, horseradish, mustard, and black pepper. Add more horseradish, mustard, and pepper to taste. Cover and chill mixture overnight. When ready to serve, place the cream cheese on a serving plate and pour the apricot mixture over the cream cheese. Serve with your favorite crackers.

Avocado SLICES

3 ripe avocados
1/2 cup extra virgin olive oil
1/4 cup balsamic vinegar
Salt and pepper to taste

1/4 teaspoon mustard powder
1/4 teaspoon garlic powder
1/4 teaspoon red chili pepper (optional)
Parsley or cilantro, chopped

Chill the avocados, then pare and slice them. In a small bowl, combine olive oil, vinegar, salt, pepper, mustard powder, garlic powder, and chili pepper; stir well. Marinate the avocado slices with the mixture, and let stand for 5 minutes. Sprinkle the tops of the slices with the chopped parsley or cilantro.

Fresh Garden VEGETABLE DIP

1 cup sour cream
²⁄₃ cup mayonnaise
1½ tablespoons green onions, diced and shredded
1½ tablespoons parsley, minced

1½ tablespoons dill weed, minced
1 tablespoon all-purpose seasoning
½ tablespoon peeled garlic, finely minced (optional)

In a medium bowl, blend the sour cream and mayonnaise. Add remaining ingredients; stir well. Chill for at least one hour to allow all of the flavors to blend. Place the bowl of dip in the center of a serving tray surrounded by cut carrots, broccoli, cauliflower, celery, and tomatoes.

Hot Pepper VEGETABLE DIP

1 cup sour cream
¼ cup milk
1 (8-ounce) package cream
    cheese, softened
¼ cup chopped olives

1 tablespoon green onion, sliced
1 cup Hot Pepper Monterey Jack
    cheese, shredded
1 (2-ounce) jar diced pimientos, drained
¼ teaspoon hot pepper sauce

In a small bowl, combine sour cream, milk, and cream cheese. Beat with an electric hand mixer, on medium speed, for 2–3 minutes or until smooth. Stir in the remaining ingredients. Cover and refrigerate for 2–3 hours before serving. Serve with carrot sticks, broccoli, cauliflower, celery, green pepper strips, and red pepper strips.

Christmas VEGETABLE WREATH

2 large bunches curly leaf parsley
2 cups celery stalks
2 cups cauliflower florets
2 pints cherry tomatoes

20 radishes
2 cups broccoli florets
2 cups baby carrots
1 large cucumber, peeled and sliced

Choose a large round serving plate with a slightly raised rim. Make a bed around the edge of the plate with half of the parsley, making sure to leave enough room for a bowl of dip in the center of the wreath. Arrange the vegetables in the parsley, filling in gaps with the remaining parsley as needed. If you have extra vegetables, set them aside and replenish the wreath as it gets eaten.

Vegetable PIZZA

2 (8-ounce) cans refrigerated
    crescent roll dough
2 (8-ounce) packages cream
    cheese, softened
1 cup mayonnaise
1 package ranch dressing mix

1 cup carrots, chopped
1 cup broccoli, chopped
1 cup cauliflower, chopped
1 (8-ounce) package shredded
    cheddar cheese

Preheat oven to 350 degrees. Spray a 12x18-inch pan with nonstick cooking spray. Unroll crescent roll dough. Press dough into the bottom of the prepared pan. Press the edges up to form a crust. Bake dough until it is firm, about 8–10 minutes. Allow to cool. Use an electric hand mixer to blend the cream cheese, mayonnaise, and ranch dressing mix. Spread the mixture over the baked crust. Sprinkle carrots, broccoli, cauliflower, and cheese over the dressing mixture. Refrigerate for at least 2 hours before serving.

Italian VEGETABLE DIP

1 cup sour cream
1 cup mayonnaise
1 (6-ounce) package Italian
   dressing mix

¼ cup red pepper, finely chopped
¼ cup green pepper, finely chopped

In a small bowl, combine sour cream, mayonnaise, and dressing mix. Stir until well blended and smooth. Add peppers and stir until well combined. Chill in the refrigerator before serving. Serve with chilled, cut vegetables.

O little town of Bethlehem,
how still we see thee lie!
Above thy deep and dreamless sleep
the silent stars go by.
Yet in thy dark streets shineth
the everlasting Light;
The hopes and fears of all the years
are met in thee tonight.

PHILLIPS BROOKS

Glory to God in the highest,
and on earth peace,
good will toward men.

LUKE 2:14